WITHDRAWN

The Story of Science

The Mystery of Gravity

by Barry Parker

BENCHMARK BOOKS

MARSHALL CAVENDISH
NEW YORK

Series Editor: Roy A. Gallant

Series Consultants:

LIFE SCIENCES
Dr. Edward J. Kormondy
Chancellor and Professor of Biology (retired)
University of Hawaii-Hilo/West Oahu

PHYSICAL SCIENCES
Dr. Jerry LaSala
Department of Physics
University of Southern Maine

Benchmark Books
Marshall Cavendish
99 White Plains Road
Tarrytown, NY 10591-9001

Library of Congress Cataloging-in-Publication Data
Parker, Barry.
    The mystery of gravity / by Barry Parker.
        p. cm. — (The story of science)
Includes bibliographical references and index.
Summary: Defines gravity and discusses how our knowledge of the natural force has broadened and evolved.
ISBN 0-7614-1428-2
    1. Gravity—Juvenile literature. 2. Gravitation—Juvenile literature.
[1. Gravity.] I. Title. II. Series.
  QC178 .P29 2003   531'.14—dc21   2002000970

Photo research by Linda Sykes Picture Research, Hilton Head, SC
Diagrams on pp. 8–9, 25, 30, 33, 34–35, 45, 47, 48–49, 54, 56, 64–65, 66 by Ian Warpole

Title page: If you were approaching a black hole in a spaceship it would look like a circular region of the sky in which there were no stars. The black hole gives off no light but it blocks the light of stars behind it. If you got too close to the black hole, its strong gravitation would pull you into it. Once inside there would be no escape. Black holes are, indeed, one of nature's strangest creations.

Cover: Sally Bensusen/Science Photo Library/Photo Researchers, Inc.
Photo Credits: Aaron Horowitz/Corbis: 1; The Granger Collection: 7, 10, 13, 14–15, 17, 18–19, 21, 23, 24, 28–29, 39, 51; Photo Researchers, Inc.: 29 (inset); Hulton/Getty Images: 32, 42–43, 68; NASA/Photo Researchers, Inc.: 59, 60–61; Sally Bensusen/Science Photo Library/Photo Researchers, Inc, 70–71; photo by Mark Godfrey, Courtesy Vera Rubin: 72.

Cover design by Bob O'Brien

Printed in Hong Kong
6 5 4 3 2 1

To David and Gloria

Contents

One

Crystal Spheres and Epicycles

During the golden age of Greek culture, around 500 B.C., men of great knowledge, called philosophers, sought answers to many questions about Earth and the Universe. They wondered about the planets, the Sun, and the Moon. Why did they seem to move the way they did? What were their shapes? Such questions led them to devise models of the Universe, but they were models that lacked even a hint of *gravity*. What, then, held their models and their notions of the Universe together?

Pythagoras, Plato, and Eudoxus

One of the earliest Greek philosophers was Pythagoras, who lived from about 560 B.C. to 480 B.C. Like many of the early

Early civilizations had strange views of the Universe. In this Hindu view, a giant tortoise known as Akupara supports elephants, upon which Earth rests. The whole is enclosed by the serpent, Asootee.

philosophers, Pythagoras's major interest was numbers. To him the numbers 1 and 10 were sacred. At the time, only seven heavenly bodies and Earth were known. Pythagoras was convinced there had to be ten, and when he set up his model of the Universe it had ten bodies in it. Instead of placing Earth at the center, however, as Earth appeared to be the central point around which the heavens turned, the center was occupied by what he called the "central fire." No one could see this fire because another body, which Pythagoras called the counter-earth, blocked the view.

Another important early Greek philosopher was Plato. About 390 B.C. he set up an academy of learning in a suburb of the Greek city of Athens, a beautiful place surrounded by olive

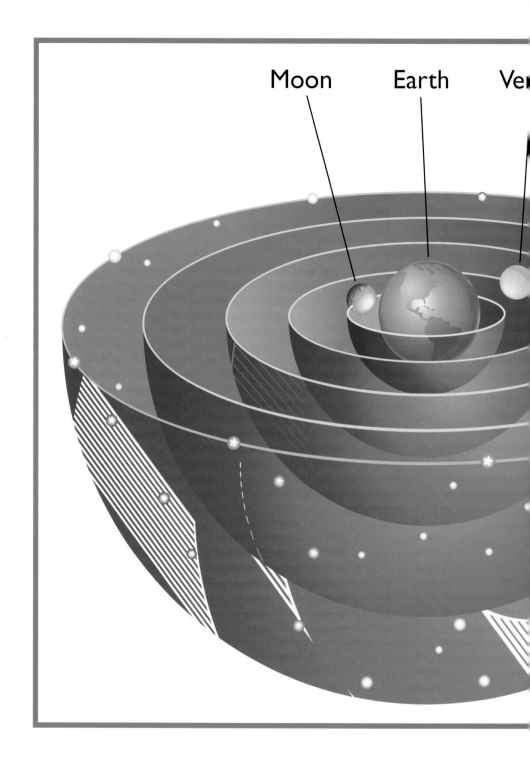

Moon   Earth   Ve

Mars

Attached to the invisible spheres of Eudoxus were the planets, the Moon, and the Sun—one to each sphere. Earth was assumed to be at the center. Each sphere had its separate axis, so they rotated in different directions, but were connected to one another. The outermost sphere held the fixed stars.

trees. Like Pythagoras, Plato loved numbers and geometry. He respected them so much that above the main door to the academy he placed the sign "Let None but Geometers Enter Here."

Although Plato spent little time observing the heavens, he was fascinated by them. To him the heavens were an arena of perfection. The heavenly bodies, therefore, had to have the perfect shape of spheres. He put Earth at the center of his model with the other heavenly bodies orbiting it in perfect circles. It was a simple model with many things not explained, but important changes would soon be made by two of Plato's students.

The first to modify his model was Eudoxus. We know little about his early life except that he lived about 370 B.C. and as a young man came to Plato's academy, where he stayed for most of his life. Although impressed with Plato and his model of the Universe, he soon saw that there was a problem: It didn't explain *how* the planets moved. To overcome this, Eudoxus introduced the idea of crystal spheres. These were huge spheres that carried each of the planets, the Sun, and the Moon around in their orbits. Each body was attached to its own crystal sphere. The outermost one, called the celestial sphere, contained all the stars. In all, his model had twenty-seven nesting crystal spheres, one inside the other with Earth at the center.

The early Greek philosopher Aristotle (384–322 B.C.) had strange ideas about Earth's elements. He thought there were four: earth, water, air, and fire. He also believed that heavy objects fell faster than light ones. All of his ideas were not wrong; for example, he believed Earth was round.

Gravitation was not needed in Eudoxus's model because each sphere was attached to the sphere beyond it, which meant there was no danger of a sphere shifting or falling. In addition, the outer sphere drove all the others, so no explanation was needed for their combined motion. The motion of the outermost sphere was believed to be a natural motion. Eudoxus's model was ingenious for the time, but it did not account for the apparent backward movement of the planets from time to time or variations in brightness.

Aristotle, another of Plato's students, tried his hand at solving the problems he found with the spheres of Eudoxus. Many consider Aristotle the greatest of the ancient Greek philosophers. For nearly two thousand years scholars looked on him as the final authority on nearly all matters. During his life, few disputed him. Aristotle and other scholars of the time reasoned that all matter on Earth was composed of the four "elements": earth, water, air, and fire. In most cases matter was a mixture of these so-called elements. The element earth was the heaviest, water next, then air, with fire the lightest. The word gravity originally meant heaviness, so earth had the most gravity and fire the least. Indeed, according to Aristotle, fire had *antigravity* or levitation. This is why it rose to the heavens.

Each of the four elements had its natural place. As the heaviest element, earth was the lowest, water next, then air, and finally fire, as the lightest, was the highest. Natural motions on Earth occurred when each element tried to find its natural place. A stone, for example, was earth, and its natural place was the center of Earth, or as close to the center as it could get. So if you raised a stone through air and dropped it, it would fall through the air and take its natural place. No force was needed for this motion. It achieved it "naturally." But forces did come into play in certain cases. If you rolled a ball along the ground, it would move for a while, then stop. This was a forced motion and was thought to be different from a natural motion. Some things moved upward to reach their natural place. Bubbles rose through water to take their natural place above the water, and fire rose through air to find its natural place.

According to Aristotle, however, the heavenly bodies were different from Earth substances. They were composed of what he called a "fifth essence." Aristotle believed that the natural motion of the fifth essence was to move in perfect circles about the center of the Universe, unlike the other four elements, which moved vertically toward or away from the center. It was taken for granted, of course, that the center of the Universe was Earth.

Aristotle had no interest in experimenting to test many of the things he stated. It would have taken only simple experiments to test some of them, but he didn't take the time. He stated, for example, that heavy objects fell faster than light objects. He came to this conclusion by noticing that a feather fell at a slower rate than a stone. On the basis of this he stated that a 10-pound (4.5 kg) stone fell ten times faster that a 1-pound (0.5 kg) stone. This would have been very easy to disprove, but he didn't bother. Although the idea of gravity was vaguely introduced on Earth, it still played no role in the heavens.

Hipparchus and Ptolemy

Hipparchus, who lived around 150 B.C., was one the greatest of the ancient Greek astronomers. He set up an observatory on the island of Rhodes and published a catalog showing the position of 850 stars. He also reduced the number of crystal spheres—fifty-five in Aristotle's model of the Universe—to seven. Hipparchus made many important advances. Besides his star catalog, he invented several instruments for measuring the positions of stars, and he classified stars according to their *apparent brightness*, or how bright they appeared to the eye.

The last of the Greek astronomers was Ptolemy, who lived around A.D. 150. Much of what is known about Greek astronomy has come to us from Ptolemy's writings. He accepted Hipparchus's Earth-centered Solar System and even added to it. Though his model became very cumbersome, fairly accurate predictions of the planets' future positions in the sky could be made by using it.

Today, we may smile at some of the ideas of the ancient Greeks, but their Earth-centered system was really quite ingenious. Indeed, it stood for fourteen hundred years, far longer than our present Sun-centered system has been in use.

After Ptolemy, science entered what is called the Dark Ages, which lasted until about the year 1400. Few advances in astronomy

While the muse of Astronomy looks on, Ptolemy is using an early instrument of astronomy called a quadrant to measure how far the Moon is above the horizon. This is a woodcut from the year 1508.

were made during this time. Islamic astronomers made a few contributions, but most importantly, they managed to preserve the books of Ptolemy and eventually translated them into Arabic.

As science entered the Dark Ages, scholars continued to regard the heavens and Earth as separate realms, each with different natural laws. With the planets, Sun, and Moon firmly attached to crystal spheres, there was no need for a notion of gravitation. However, significant changes were soon to come.

Arabic astronomers are using simple astronomical instruments to make measurements in the sky. This is a woodcut from the year 1513.

Two

The New Astronomy

For almost a thousand years after Ptolemy's death, few advances in science were made. Then, near the end of the fifteenth century, Nicolaus Copernicus was born, and soon a new age of discovery began. Copernicus was born on February 19, 1473, in Toruń, Poland. Astronomers still had no idea of what held the Sun, Moon, and planets in place, or what made them move. Although Copernicus did not provide an answer, he did make an advance that would one day allow other scientists to understand gravity.

Copernicus: A New Home for the Sun

Copernicus was an excellent mathematician and soon became

The Polish astronomer Nicolaus Copernicus (1473–1543) proposed that the Sun, not Earth, was the center of the Solar System, a view that we now know is correct. He assumed that Earth, the other planets, and the Moon moved in perfect circles around the Sun. We now know they actually travel in elliptical orbits that are very close in form to circles.

interested in Ptolemy's system of the Universe, in which the Sun and the planets circled Earth. When he studied Ptolemy's calculations of the future positions of the planets, he saw that something was wrong. Ptolemy's predicted positions were not in agreement with the actual positions. His system also seemed

needlessly complicated, and Copernicus was sure that it could be simplified.

He decided to try a system with the Sun, rather than Earth, at the center and then tried to support it using mathematics. He found that the newly predicted positions of the planets were still not in agreement with observation, but they were closer. Copernicus was so concerned about what others would say about this Sun-centered system that he waited until he was near death before he allowed his ideas to be published. But few people paid any attention to them. It would be many years before they would be widely accepted.

Kepler: Questions and an Answer

One of the first to take Copernicus's model seriously was a mathematician named Johannes Kepler. He was born in a small town near the Black Forest in Germany in 1571, twenty-eight years after Copernicus died. As a boy, he was sickly. In addition, smallpox crippled his hand and left him with poor eyesight. Nevertheless, he attended university,

The Copernican Universe with the Sun at the center. Copernicus is shown at the lower right and Ptolemy at the lower left.

where he studied mathematics under Professor Michael Maestlin, who accepted Copernican theory.

Kepler also began to consider a number of questions that astronomers before him had not thought about seriously, if at all: Why were things in space the way they were? What made the Moon and planets move? Why didn't they fall to Earth when they were overhead? Did the planets have weight, in the way things on Earth did? Were they hollow or solid? He finally concluded that the Sun was the source of some invisible force that moved the planets, as if long fingers stretched out from the Sun and pushed them along. He referred to it as a "whirling" or "motor" force.

Kepler was familiar with magnets and the force they exerted. At one stage he wondered if the Sun's force in causing the planets to move might be magnetic. But if it were, he reasoned, then it would affect magnets here on Earth, and it didn't. He realized that the force, whatever it was, weakened with distance. Many years earlier Copernicus had shown that Mercury moved along its orbit five times faster than Saturn did. Kepler felt that the reason for these speed differences had to be that the whirling force was much stronger at Mercury because Mercury was much closer to the Sun than Saturn was.

Kepler knew that before he could solve the puzzle of the planets' orbital motion around the Sun, he would need to know more details about the paths they traced.

Kepler's War with Mars

In 1596, two years after Kepler began teaching, he published his first book, *Cosmographic Mystery*. He discussed many of the ideas in it with the great Danish astronomer Tycho Brahe, and sent a copy of it to him.

Johannes Kepler (1571–1630) gave us three laws of planetary motion.
Although he failed to solve the puzzle of gravity, his laws helped in the solution.

In 1598, because of his religious beliefs, Kepler was ordered to leave his home in Graz, Austria. In desperation, he wrote to Brahe and asked for a job. Brahe was delighted to hear from Kepler and invited him to become his assistant. This was a stroke of luck for Kepler, for Brahe's many years of observing the planets were to provide Kepler with exactly the details he needed to solve the puzzle of planetary motion.

Born in 1546, Brahe was brought up by a rich uncle and later given an island on which to set up an observatory so that he could study the stars and planets. Called Uraniborg, the observatory was very well equipped with the finest instruments, and students from all over Europe flocked to work under Brahe. Brahe had a goal: to choose between Ptolemy's and Copernicus's theories based on careful observation of the planets' motions. Over the years he gathered a large number of records of the positions, movements, and apparent brightness of each planet at various times.

On Brahe's death in 1601, Kepler inherited all of his records. He began to solve the planetary motion puzzle by working with Brahe's observations of Mars. He called it his "war with Mars." Kepler was sure he would be able to solve the problem of Mars's orbit in a few weeks. Eight years later he was still working on it.

Copernicus had used circles as orbits in his model. For two thousand years the circle had been regarded as the most "perfect" form, so it seemed reasonable to think that all heavenly bodies must move in circles. But circles didn't work for Kepler. After much frustration, he finally tried an *ellipse*. To his delight it fit the observations perfectly, and he was later able to show that all the planets move in elliptical orbits. This discovery became known as Kepler's First Law of Planetary

Over many years Tycho Brahe (1546–1601) accumulated very accurate data on the positions of the planets. Kepler used this data to formulate his laws of planetary motion. These laws eventually helped solve the puzzle of gravity.

Tycho Brahe's observatory at night. It was called Uraniborg and was on the island of Hveen, between Sweden and Denmark. Brahe's numerous assistants measured the positions of the planets and stars in the sky at this observatory.

Motion. It says that "a planet moves around the Sun in an ellipse that has the Sun as one focus."

An ellipse is roughly an oval-shaped curve. More exactly, it is the curve you get when you slice a plane through a cone at an angle, making sure you don't go through the base. Ellipses vary in shape, depending on where you slice the cone. Some are more elongated than others, and some are very close to being circles. The orbits of Mars and the other planets are actually so close to being circles that, without careful measurement, it is hard to tell they aren't circles.

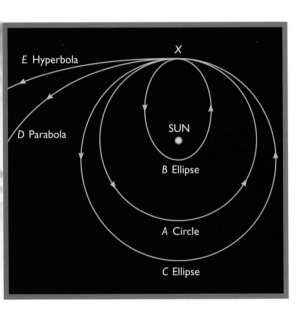

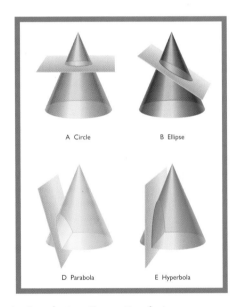

Orbital paths with conic sections: The gravitational attraction acting between the Sun and the planets holds the planets gravitational captives of the Sun. Each planet, at its particular distance from the Sun, has just the right speed to hold it in an elliptical orbit (B and C) around the Sun. Many comets travel at such high speeds that, although attracted by the Sun, they travel in open orbits, such as a parabola or a hyperbola (D and E), zooming past the Sun once, never to return. Slicing a cone at different angles produces the different orbital shapes.

The "Secret" of Gravity

As Kepler continued to work on his model of planetary motion, he became even more convinced that the force from the Sun became weaker with distance. If so, this would affect the speed of the planets as they circled the Sun. He was finally able to show mathematically that the speed of a planet increases as it gets closer to the Sun, and becomes slower when it moves farther away. This change in speed is known as Kepler's Second Law of Planetary Motion. It is also called the Law of Equal Areas. Twenty years later, Kepler published his third law, called the Harmonic Law, showing that the *period* of a planet, or the time it takes to go around the Sun, was related to its average distance from the Sun. These three laws are now a basic part of astronomy.

We now know that Kepler's three laws held the "secret" to gravity, but Kepler wasn't able to see it. Two other important ideas, which were to come later, were needed to arrive at a workable law of gravitation. Nevertheless, Kepler came remarkably close and paved the way for one of the great scientists of all time, the English scientist Isaac Newton.

Kepler died in 1630 on the edge of poverty. After a long and trying trip on horseback to collect some overdue wages, he fell ill and died. He was buried in a graveyard near Regensburg, Bavaria. The graveyard was leveled three years later. Today there is nothing to mark the gravesite of one of the world's greatest scientists.

Strangely, Kepler paid little attention to motion and gravity on Earth. This was left to the Italian Galileo Galilei, who lived about the same time as Kepler.

Three

Galileo's Gravity

Galileo Galilei, who is usually referred to only by his first name, was born in Pisa, Italy, on February 15, 1564, seven years before Kepler. He attended schools in both Pisa and Florence, and at seventeen entered the University of Pisa. Although more interested in mathematics and science, he studied medicine because that is what his father wanted him to do. After two years he was allowed to change to mathematics and science, but family finances forced him to leave school before he could earn his degree.

Galileo's love for learning continued, however, and for the next four years he studied on his own. He spent much of his time inventing new devices and building instruments. In 1586, for example, he published a small booklet describing a water balance for weighing objects. Some of his devices were so ingenious that they attracted the attention of a nobleman who managed to get him a position at the University of Pisa. So, four years after he left without a degree, he was back as a teacher.

Early Ideas about Gravity

Galileo was a popular teacher, and his classes were well attended. He soon came to think that many of Aristotle's ideas were ridiculous, and he began scoffing at them in his classes. The students liked his antics, but the other teachers were not amused to hear the great Aristotle ridiculed, and soon many of them turned against Galileo.

Years earlier, as a teenager, he had noticed something odd at the Cathedral of Pisa. A lamp that hung from the ceiling on a long chain was swinging in a way that caught Galileo's interest. Since there were no watches in his time, he used his pulse to time the swings. He noticed that regardless of how far the

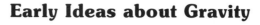

Galileo was the first scientist to consider the idea of gravitation seriously, and the first known to turn a telescope to the heavens. In 1610, Galileo showed the four tiny moons that were orbiting Jupiter to a group of Venetians. Through the telescope, they could see that everything in the Solar System didn't revolve around the Sun, as was widely believed at the time.

29

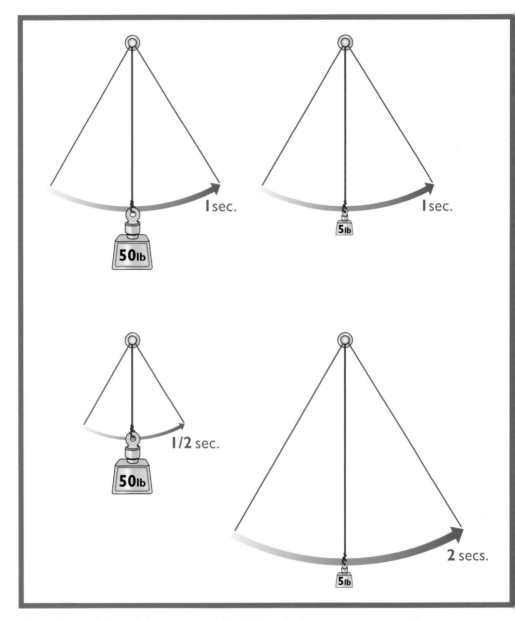

A simple pendulum of the type used by Galileo. In the top view we see that the time of the swing does not depend on the weight on the end of the string. The time is the same regardless of the weight. In the bottom view we see that the time of the swing does depend on the length of the string. The longer the string the longer it takes for a complete swing.

lamp swung from the center, the time of the swing was the same. Today we call such a swinging object a pendulum.

As Galileo's interest in pendulums grew, he began to experiment at home. He attached a weight to a rope and tied the other end to a high point. He found that not only did the length of the swing have no effect on the time of the swing, but the weight on the end also made no difference. He tied together rocks of several different weights and found that the swing time was always the same. The only thing that mattered was the length of the rope. This surprised him and started him thinking about the force that moved a pendulum—gravity.

Aristotle's Fable and Galileo's Logic

Aristotle had taught that heavier objects fell faster than lighter ones. That idea was accepted for hundreds of years, but Galileo was skeptical. According to an early account, he dropped balls of different weights all at once from the Leaning Tower of Pisa and saw that they all fell to the ground at the same time. However, it is unlikely that Galileo actually did this. Among other things, the experiment had already been done in 1586 by Simon Stevin in Holland. He soon realized that the difference in the rate at which objects fell was due to air resistance, not weight. If the object was flat, like a sheet of paper, air slowed it down as it fell. This is why a feather and a marble fall at different rates. If you put them in a vacuum, however, they will fall at the same rate. Because Galileo wasn't able to create a vacuum, he couldn't demonstrate his point through experimentation.

You can easily test the effect of air resistance. Take a marble and a sheet of paper and drop them both at the same time. The marble will hit the ground well before the piece of paper. Now crunch the paper tightly until it is a small ball.

The Italian astronomer Galileo Galilei measured the time it took for a ball to roll down an incline. He showed that, neglecting air resistance, heavy objects do not fall faster than light ones, as believed by Aristotle. Legend had it that he dropped balls of unequal weights from the Leaning Tower of Pisa, but he probably did not really do that.

When you drop both objects again, you will see that they fall at about the same rate.

Because Galileo tested so many of his ideas by performing experiments, he became known as the father of experimental science. But he also applied logic and common sense to arrive at many of his conclusions. For example, he imagined the following thought experiment. Assume you drop a bowling ball and time how long it takes to fall to the ground. Then you cut it in half. Each part of the ball will then weigh only half as much as the original ball. Since each half is much lighter, both should fall at a slower rate, according to Aristotle. Galileo realized there was something wrong with this logic.

Rolling Balls

Galileo could use his pulse as a watch, or even a crude water clock that was driven by the flow of water, but neither was very precise. He would somehow have to slow down his falling objects so he could time them more accurately, but how? He hit on the idea of rolling balls down ramps or inclines. Gravity would still act on them, and he could measure its effect better. He noticed that

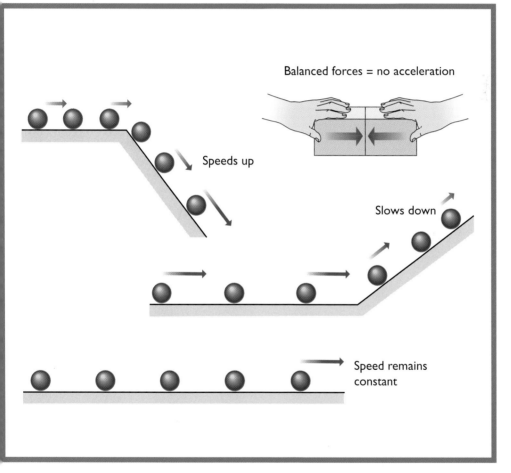

A ball rolling down an incline speeds up due to the action of gravity. A ball rolling up an incline slows down. A ball rolling on the level would continue with constant speed if it were not for friction slowing it down.

each ball rolled down the ramp in the same amount of time, no matter what it was made of or how heavy it was. Furthermore, each ball speeded up, or *accelerated*, in the same way.

Although Galileo could not measure the *acceleration of gravity* precisely, today we know it accurately. An object dropped from a high tower falls at a speed of 32 feet (10 m) per second at the end of the first second, 64 feet (20 m) per second at the end of the second second, and 96 feet (29 m) per second at the end of the third. We can also measure how far it falls during each of these seconds. In 1 second it falls 16 feet (5 m), in two seconds 64 feet (20 m), and in 3 seconds 144 feet (44 m). It is easy to see from these numbers that the object's speed increases rapidly as it falls.

Galileo discovered something else about falling objects. If you drop one object and throw another, such as a pitched ball, parallel

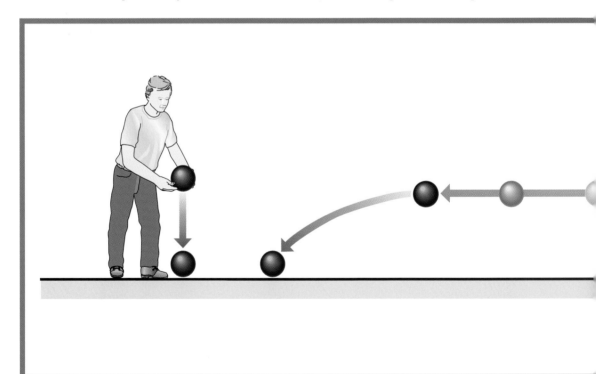

to the ground at the same time, they both fall at the same rate and strike the ground at the same time. This means that forward speed over the ground does not change the effect of gravity.

Gravity and Inertia

Galileo was bothered by something. Why did a heavy object fall at the same rate as a light one? To understand why it seemed odd to him, let's do another thought-experiment. Assume that we have four balls that weigh: 10 pounds (5 kg), 5 pounds (2 kg), 2 pounds (.9 kg), and 1 pound (.5 kg). We arrange for helpers and we drop all four balls at once. As expected, they all hit the ground at the same time.

Now, put all four balls on a level floor and give each a push with the same force. You will find that the heaviest ball goes the

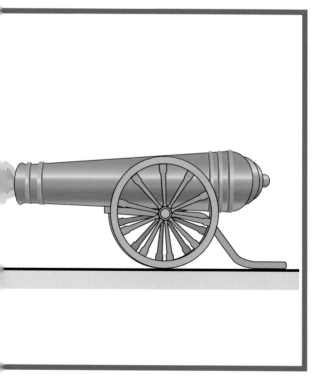

As hard as it is to believe, a cannonball shot horizontally strikes the ground at the same time as a cannonball dropped from the height of the cannon.

slowest. Each of the lighter balls rolls faster, depending on its weight, or *mass* (how much matter it contains). This means that the lighter the ball, the greater its acceleration for the same force.

Although we apply the same force to each ball, the acceleration of each is different. But when gravity, instead of our muscles, does the work, the balls all move at the same rate. This means that gravity must somehow apply a greater force on the heavier balls than on the lighter ones, and indeed it does. But how can gravity "know" how much an object weighs?

For an answer, we have to look to *inertia*. Galileo knew something about inertia, but he didn't understand it very well. We know that inertia is resistance to change in motion. For example, it takes more muscle power to push a stalled car than it takes to push a scooter because the car has more mass. The reason all objects fall at the same rate is because it is harder for gravity to overcome a heavier object's inertia, just as it is harder to push a car than a scooter. Gravity pulls heavier objects with a greater force, but inertia resists with a greater effect. If an object weighs 10 pounds (5 kg), for example, the force of gravity on it is ten times greater than it is on an object weighing 1 pound (.5 kg). But its inertia is also ten times as great, so it falls at the same rate as the 1 pound (.5 kg) object.

Gravity and the Heavens

Galileo was not well known before he was forty-five years old, in 1609. Although he had written a few books, he was not famous, but his use of the telescope would bring him fame. The telescope was invented in the Netherlands in 1608. Galileo heard of the invention and soon made his own telescopes. He became the first person to study the Moon, Jupiter, the Milky Way, and other objects in the sky. What he saw astounded both him and those he invited to look through his "optik tube." His enemies, however, either refused to look or refused to believe what they saw, saying that Galileo had bewitched his telescopes. One of the most important of his observations was the motion of Jupiter's four largest moons. This was the first time anyone had ever seen objects in the sky that did not seem to be moving around Earth. According to Ptolemy's system, everything revolved around Earth.

Interestingly, Galileo never related those motions to gravity. He was mainly interested in motion and gravity on Earth, thinking that once he understood how they worked here he could then apply his knowledge to the heavens, but he never did. This was left to Isaac Newton, who was born in 1642, the year Galileo died.

Early on, Galileo became convinced that the Copernican system was the correct one, with the Sun at the center of the Solar System and all the planets revolving around it. He was very outspoken about his belief, even though it went against the teachings of the Catholic Church, which was then a very powerful social force. When he talked to the pope about his beliefs, the pope was sympathetic but argued against him. Galileo later wrote a book in which he put the pope's arguments in the mouth of a not-too-bright philosopher named Simplicio. The pope was outraged and eventually Galileo was put on trial and forced to publicly recant his beliefs. He was seventy years old by this time and spent the remaining seven years of his life under house arrest. Despite his troubles with the church, Galileo was a devout Catholic and did not intentionally anger the pope. He just did not seem to understand why his words would make the pope react as he did because he was writing as a scientist.

Galileo made important contributions to our understanding of gravity. He discovered many of the basic laws of motion and of falling bodies, and he made important discoveries with his telescope.

Four

The Apple Must Fall

Although Isaac Newton did not invent gravity, he discovered and explained how it works. He showed that, without gravity, all of the planets and their moons would go flying off into space. His work marked one of the most important scientific discoveries of all time.

Newton was born in Woolsthorpe, England, on Christmas Day, 1642, the same year in which Galileo died. When he was young, Newton was quiet and kept to himself much of the time. He loved to work with his hands, building windmills, sundials, and water clocks, and he loved to fly kites with lanterns in them. His mother hoped to make a farmer out of him so he could work

Sir Isaac Newton, one of the greatest scientists of all time, worked out his first universal law of gravitation. According to this law, all objects in the Universe attract one another with a force that depends on the mass and distance between the objects. Through this law, the motions of the planets and other heavenly objects were understood for the first time.

the family farm, but soon it was obvious that he would never be good at it. She would often find him reading a book behind a hedge when he was supposed to be working. One of his teachers saw that young Newton had a talent for mathematics and science and encouraged his mother to let him attend Cambridge University instead of working the farm. She was reluctant at first but eventually gave in.

At Cambridge, Newton took the usual courses but he did not stand out in any way. In 1664, at the age of twenty-three, he graduated with a bachelor's degree, but his further education was interrupted when all the students were sent home because of an outbreak of the Black Plague. He spent the next two years back at the farm, and they became the most creative years of his life. During this time, he pondered the laws of motion and many of the properties of light. He also invented an important branch of

Newton's Laws of Motion

FIRST LAW: A body remains at rest or, if in motion, remains in uniform motion with constant speed in a straight line, unless it is acted upon by a force.

SECOND LAW: The acceleration produced by a force depends on the magnitude of the force and on the mass of the body.

THIRD LAW: For every action there is an equal and opposite reaction.

mathematics called calculus. He soon published his discoveries about calculus, but did not publish his ideas about optics, motion, and gravity until many years later.

Discovery of the Law of Gravity

One of the most important events in Newton's life is supposed to have occurred during this long vacation from school. By this time, Newton had been puzzling over the question of what makes the planets move as they do. Like Kepler, he realized that a force must be acting on the planets, but unlike Kepler, he had the advantage of his own three laws of motion to help him figure out the nature of that force. Thanks to Newton's first law, he realized that Kepler's idea that a "whirling" force must be pushing the planets around in their orbits was incorrect. Rather, a force must be pulling the planets toward the Sun; otherwise, they would fly away in straight lines and never be seen again. In the same way, a force must pull the Moon toward Earth. It seemed likely that it was the same force in both cases.

By combining his own second law with Kepler's third law, Newton was able to figure out a mathematical solution to how the mysterious force weakened with distance. But what could the force be?

Newton was pondering these questions on his family's farm while he waited out the Plague. One day, the story has it, he noticed an apple falling from a tree. (We are not sure if this story is true, or if it is like the story of George Washington and the cherry tree, but it is certain that Newton figured out the law of gravity at this time.) This gave him an idea. The falling apple accelerated, which meant a force must be pulling it toward the ground (according to his own second law). Today, we know that force as gravity. What if this were the same force that pulls the Moon

toward Earth? That idea marked the beginning of Newton's discovery.

First, he knew how the planetary force decreased with increasing distance. Second, he knew the distance to the Moon pretty well, since it had been measured as long ago as 250 B.C. By putting those two bits of information together, he could calculate how strong gravity would be at the Moon's distance. He found that the result agreed pretty well with the force his second law said would be needed to keep the Moon in its orbit. So Newton did not need a mysterious planetary force to control the planets. Ordinary gravity was enough.

Newton was a perfectionist, and he did not want to share his discovery until he was absolutely sure of it. For almost twenty years he kept it a secret as he worked out the details. He found that his gravity idea explained all three of Kepler's laws of planetary motion. The need to convince himself that his calculations were accurate led him to invent calculus. Everything worked. Gravity was the force that made his planets move as they do.

The Woolsthorpe home of Isaac Newton as it is today. This is where he spent his youth and where he presumably watched an apple fall. This led him to formulate his universal law of gravitation.

Other Discoveries

In 1667 Newton returned to Cambridge, where he continued to work on his experiments. Two years later his favorite teacher retired and Newton took over his position. Newton was not a popular teacher. Few students, sometimes none at all, attended his lectures, but this didn't bother him. He would trudge back to his study and continue working on his research.

During this time, Newton made more discoveries, such as the optical properties of lenses and light, but he did not tell anyone about them. New discoveries were generally announced at the meetings of a scientific society called the Royal Society. Newton eventually reported some of his discoveries to the society, but one of the members, Robert Hooke, criticized him so much that he eventually stopped reporting them. He was very sensitive to criticism and almost childish in his reaction to it. For many years, therefore, all his important discoveries, including his work on gravitation, remained secret on scraps of paper in his study.

Earth–Moon Tug of War

When a rocket ship flies to the Moon, it must be launched with enough speed to escape Earth's gravity. After reaching that speed and increasing its distance from Earth, the ship then goes slower as Earth keeps tugging on it. That tends to hold it back, just as it does to a ball tossed straight up into the air.

But all the while, as the distance between Earth and the ship keeps increasing, Earth's gravitational tug weakens. Eventually, the ship reaches a point beyond the halfway mark where the Moon's gravity is just as strong as Earth's. The point is called L-1, named after the famous

At blastoff, a rocket ship is given enough speed to escape Earth's gravity and coast to the Moon, but Earth's gravity starts to slow it down as it moves. At L-1, the Moon's lesser gravity exactly balances Earth's stronger gravity. As it goes through L-1, the Moon's gravity becomes stronger than Earth's and the ship is pulled toward the Moon. Since Earth's gravity is stronger than the Moon's, the L-1 point is closer to the Moon rather than midway between it and Earth.

French mathematician Joseph-Louis Lagrange, who worked out the mathematics before he died in 1813.

On coasting through the L-1 point, the ship is next speeded up because the Moon's gravitational tug on the ship now grows stronger as the ship gets closer to the Moon.

When it is time to return home, the rocket ship does not need as much speed to escape the Moon's weaker gravity because its mass is smaller than Earth's. When the ship reaches and coasts through the L-1 point again, Earth's gravity takes over and speeds the ship home.

Rediscovery of Newton's Law of Gravitation

One day in 1684 three members of the Royal Society were having lunch together. One of them was Edmond Halley, after whom the famous Halley's comet is named. The three men began talking about Kepler's laws of planetary motion and wondered how they might be explained. They were sure that the force that kept the planets in orbit around the Sun was the same as the force that kept the Moon in orbit around Earth. But there were many questions. How exactly did this force work? What was the shape of the Moon's orbit? Could it be calculated?

Halley offered a prize to anyone who could answer those questions within two months, but no one claimed it. The problem was obviously very difficult. Halley was sure, however, that there was one person who could solve it: Isaac Newton. Visiting him at Cambridge, Halley asked, "What would the shape of the orbit be for a force that dropped off as distance increased?"

"An ellipse," Newton replied without hesitation.

"How do you know?" Halley asked in surprise.

"Because I solved the problem many years ago," Newton said.

Halley asked if he could see the calculation. Newton looked for it, but his study was in such a mess that he couldn't find the scraps of paper on which the solution was written. He promised to send it to Halley, and three months later he did. This time his calculations produced a more accurate result for the Moon's orbital period, since the Moon's distance had been determined more accurately. Newton also showed how all three of Kepler's laws could be explained by a universal law of gravitation.

Halley was overjoyed. Newton had shown without a doubt that gravity was a force that existed between all objects in the Universe. The force that pulled the apple to the ground was the same force that also held the Moon in its orbit around Earth, and the planets in their orbits around the Sun. And it was the force of gravity that caused the paths of the planets to be curved away from a straight line. But if this were so, why wasn't Earth's path through space curved by the Moon's gravity? As it turns out, it is. But Earth is so much heavier, or more

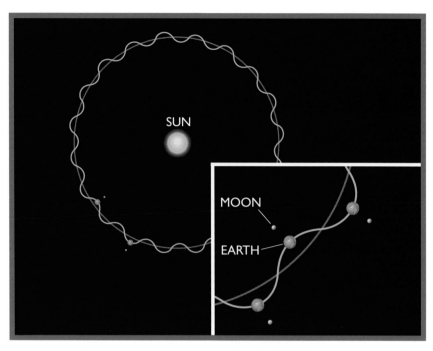

The Moon's gravitational tug on Earth causes Earth to trace a wobbly path around the Sun. The inset shows how the Moon's position in orbit around Earth pulls Earth off course to the left or right. Astronomers can detect the presence of unseen planets circling distant stars by studying the wobbly path traced by a star with an especially massive planet circling it.

massive, and has so much more inertia that as a result its path changes very little.

Newton's law of gravitation can be stated as: *Every particle of matter (or object) in the Universe attracts every other particle of matter (or object) with a force that depends on their masses and the distance between them.*

Due to Halley's efforts, Newton's laws of motion and his universal law of gravitation were published in 1687 in a book called *Principia*. It turned out to be one of the greatest scientific books ever published. Newton purposely made it difficult to read in order to avoid criticism from those who knew little science. Still,

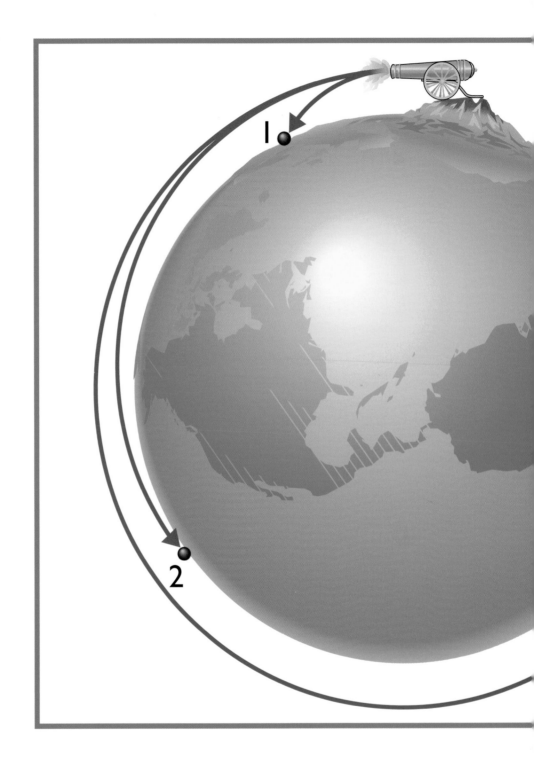

3

there were barbs to endure. His old enemy, Robert Hooke, claimed that Newton had stolen some of his ideas from him. And later the German scholar Gottfried Wilhelm Liebniz accused Newton of introducing "miracles" into science. Furthermore, some of Liebniz's friends claimed that Newton had stolen his principles of calculus from Leibniz.

Newton's law of gravitation was considered to be a tremendous breakthrough. The law made it possible for scientists to make accurate calculations of the positions of moons, planets, comets, and other astronomical objects. The planet Neptune eventually was discovered as a result of the law. Still, *Principia* did not tell us what gravity is, and how it makes itself felt across the long, empty stretches of space. Newton never claimed to know.

What is gravity? It turns out to be even stranger than anyone thought.

An illustration from Newton's Principia. *He showed that if you were on a high mountain and projected a rock or other object with moderate speed it would return to the surface of Earth. It you increased the speed, however, you would eventually reach a point where the rock would orbit Earth in either a circular or, more likely, an elliptical orbit.*

Five

Gravity as Curved Space–Time

Newton's theory was excellent. It described the motions of the planets, moons, and other celestial objects very accurately, but other problems remained. For one thing, the odd relationship between gravitation and inertia that makes all bodies fall at the same rate was not explained. And the planet Mercury did not appear to obey Newton's theory. Its motion in the heavens was slightly different from what Newton's theory had predicted. These problems were not solved for another 225 years, when Albert Einstein published a new theory of gravitation in 1915.

Albert Einstein gave us a new and different theory of gravity in 1915. He believed that mass curves space in a mysterious way. We cannot see this curvature, but when a massive object like a planet encounters it, the planet is forced to follow the curvature. A planet going around the Sun, therefore, follows the curved space created by the mass of the Sun.

Einstein as a Youth

Einstein was born in Ulm, Germany, in 1879. Although his parents worried because he was late in learning to talk, later on he was always near the top of his class in school. When he was fifteen, his family moved to Milan, Italy, leaving Albert behind to finish high school. He hated it and longed to join his family so much that he finally fled to Milan before graduating. He promised his parents, however, that he would take the entrance exams at the nearby Polytechnic in Zurich, Switzerland. If he passed he could enter the university without a high school certificate.

He took the exam that summer and failed because he was weak in botany, Latin, and Greek. His grades in mathematics and physics were so high, however, that the officials suggested that he go to a nearby town and finish his high-school education. Einstein enjoyed the school and graduated the following spring. In the autumn, he entered the university at Zurich. He preferred to work in the laboratory and study on his own, but soon found himself far behind in his class work. When the final exams came, he had to borrow a classmate's notes and narrowly passed.

For the next two years Einstein taught part time while he looked for a job. He eventually found employment at a patent office in Bern, Switzerland. His job was to look at inventions and issue patents, which protected the inventor from people who might steal his ideas. During this time, he began working on scientific problems in his spare time. He was soon to publish his first scientific paper.

First Steps Toward a New Theory of Gravity

Years earlier, Einstein had begun thinking about space and time. When he was sixteen, he wondered what it would be like to ride a beam of light, and he soon reasoned that strange things would happen. Newton had said that time was the same for all observers anywhere in the Universe. Einstein did not believe it, and in 1905 he showed that Newton was wrong. He published a theory called special relativity that surprised the scientific world. It showed that both time and space were much stranger than anyone had thought. Time, for example, depended on your motion relative to other observers. The faster you traveled relative to another observer, the slower time passed when you compared your clock to that of the other person.

Einstein's theory of special relativity was a magnificent theory, but it applied only to objects moving in a straight line at uniform speeds. Later he extended the theory to include accelerated motion, which is quite different from uniform motion. Sometimes it is difficult to tell if you are moving uniformly, especially if you are in an airplane or a large, smoothly moving ship. But you know you are accelerating when taking off in an airplane or when riding in a rapidly accelerating car because an inertial force pushes you back into your seat.

More Thought Experiments

Einstein felt that there had to be a relationship between inertia and gravity. To find out what it was, he performed a thought experiment, just as Galileo had. In his thought experiment, he was in a rocket ship with no windows. If the rocket ship were parked on Earth, Einstein knew that he would feel the force of gravity pulling him to the floor of the ship, just as if he were standing on the ground.

But next he supposed the rocket ship was out in space and accelerating at 32 feet (10 m) per second per second—the same as the acceleration of gravity on Earth. No matter in which direction the ship was accelerating, Einstein knew that if he dropped a ball, the floor would accelerate "up" to meet it. To him, of course, it would appear that the ball was "falling." Nevertheless, it would be moving at 32 feet (10 m) per second per second, the same rate at which it would fall back on Earth. But since the ball "falls" in the rocket ship, there must be a force acting on it, and since it falls at the same rate as it would on Earth, the two forces must be the same. To Einstein, this meant that the force of acceleration and the force of gravitation must be related.

What Einstein was actually experiencing in his imaginary rocket ship was *inertial force*, the force that you feel when you are in a car that accelerates, not gravitational force. Even so, to him it appeared that this inertial force and the force of gravity were exactly the same.

Einstein then considered another thought experiment. He assumed that he was still in his imaginary rocket ship out in space and that it was still accelerating. He knew that Earth has a *gravitational field*—that is, a region around it within which other objects are attracted. He reasoned, therefore, that since inertial force and the force of gravity are the same, his rocket ship must also have something called an *inertial field*. Furthermore, this inertial field should act the same as Earth's gravitational field.

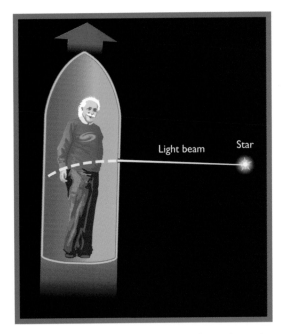

Light beam   Star

The light beam from a star enters from the right and crosses in front of Einstein. At the same time, the rocket accelerates upward and so deflects the light beam downward because the gravity and acceleration are the same.

Continuing his thought experiment, he then drilled a hole in the side of his rocket ship to let the light from a distant star shine in and cross the cabin. Because the rocket ship was accelerating, he saw that the light beam was curved downward by the rocket ship's inertial field, just as water from a hose is curved downward by Earth's gravitational field.

To Einstein's way of thinking, this meant that any gravitational field should "curve," or deflect, any beam of light. Therefore, a beam of light from a distant star should be curved a bit as it passes the Sun, since the Sun has a strong gravitational field.

Thought experiments were fine, but how could he find out if a light beam really is curved by the Sun? The only time he would be able to see if this happened would be during a total eclipse of the Sun, when the stars around it were visible. So he had to wait for an eclipse.

All this was very interesting, but Einstein also needed a mathematical equation that would tell him how much the light beam would be curved as it passed the Sun. This equation would also give him a way to determine the gravitational strength of other bodies in space. In 1915 he finally worked it out.

A New Theory of Gravity

What he worked out was his new theory of gravity, now called the general theory of relativity.

The bending of light around the edge of the Sun that Einstein predicted was finally observed during an eclipse of the Sun in 1919. Einstein soon realized, however, that it was not the light beam that was bending. It was actually space itself near the Sun that was being bent, or curved. The Sun curved the space around it, and it is this curved space that we call gravitation. So, curved space and gravity are the same thing.

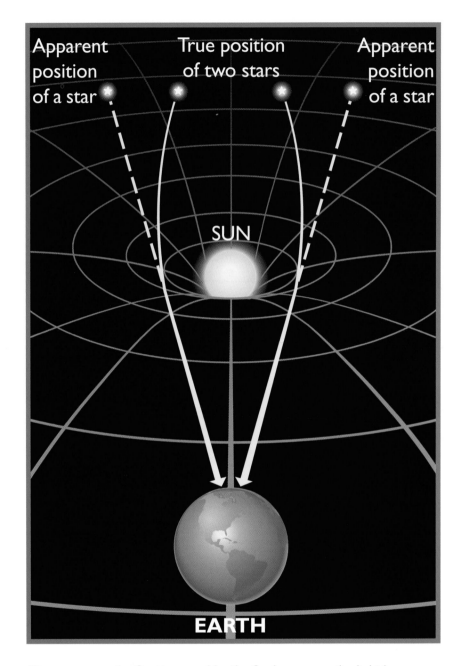

The space near the Sun is curved by the Sun's mass, so the light beam from a distant star will be deflected as it passes near the Sun. The star will not be seen in its true position, but slightly shifted.

But how can space be curved? After all, what is space but emptiness? Although no one can *see* curved space, Einstein showed mathematically that it can exist. In the world of physics there are many things and conditions that are beyond our ability to see or experience. Atoms and curved space are only two of them. The best way to imagine curved space is to think of the surface of a rubber sheet suspended in the air. If you place a heavy ball on it, its surface sags into a curve. The space around the Sun and other bodies in the Universe, such as planets and moons, is curved in much the same way. If you spin a marble around the curved part of the rubber, it will move around the heavy Sun-ball in an elliptical orbit, just as the planets actually move around the Sun.

Einstein obtained a solution to his theory but it was not as complete as he wanted it to be. As he continued to work on the problem, an astronomer named Karl Schwarzschild received a copy of Einstein's new theory while he was fighting on the Russian front during World War I. He had come down with a rare disease, and by the time he studied Einstein's paper he was weak and exhausted from his illness. Nevertheless, he solved the equation and obtained an exact solution, which he sent to Einstein. Einstein was astonished but pleased, and thanked him. Schwarzschild died soon afterward.

Einstein's theory was a remarkable piece of work and is now the accepted theory of gravitation. For example, it explains what holds the planets in orbit around the Sun and why a golf ball usually doesn't roll quite far enough, or a bit too far, on the green. But it is Einstein's theory of gravitation, and only his theory, that explains the very strange conditions that exist in the depths of space when gigantic stars collapse and crush space and time.

Where Newton regarded gravity as a force acting between any two objects in space, Einstein thought of gravity as the way mass affects the shape of space.

Six

The Strange Results of Extreme Gravity

The only gravity we can feel is Earth's. But each of the other bodies of the Solar System—the Sun, Moon, and the other planets—has a gravitational field, and each is different from that of Earth. The gravitational strength of a body depends on two things: its mass and the distance from the center of the object. The Sun, for example, is 330,000 times more massive than Earth, but it is also 110 times larger than Earth. If you could stand on the surface of the Sun, its gravitational field

A field of galaxies photographed by the Hubble Space Telescope. All these galaxies are moving away from us because of the expansion of the Universe. The farther away they are, the faster they are moving. They are also seen as they were billions of years ago because it has taken time for the light from them to reach us. Even though the Universe is expanding, it is still held together by gravity.

would be 28 times stronger than Earth's: if you weigh 75 pounds (34 kg) on Earth, you'd weigh 2,100 pounds (953 kg) on the Sun! But here on Earth we are much farther from the Sun's center and its gravitational pull is much weaker—it is only about 1/2,000 of Earth's gravitational pull on us, so we do not notice it.

Gravity's Effect on Time

Einstein showed that gravity becomes most interesting when it is extremely strong. Many strange things happen, some that most people find difficult to understand. One of the things Einstein's theory of relativity told us is that time slows down as a gravitational field grows stronger. This may seem a little crazy. How can time slow down? The best way to show that it does would be to put a clock in a very strong gravitational field, such as that of a very massive star, then watch it through a telescope and compare it to a clock beside you. Within a short time you would notice that it appears to be running slow compared to your clock.

Since Earth's gravitational field is strongest near the ground and weakens as we move farther away from it, a clock out in space runs slightly faster than a clock on Earth. Because time passes faster for someone out in space than it does for

Astronauts in the space shuttle do not feel any gravity. With a small push they float around the cabin of the shuttle. Anything that is not tacked down also floats around if it is given a slight push. This makes it difficult to eat and perform certain duties. In most cases, however, it is easier to work in space when gravity is canceled out.

someone standing on the ground, a person living in the pent-house at the top of a skyscraper ages a little faster than some-one who lives on the first floor of the building. The difference, however, is too small to notice—less than a billionth of a sec-ond in a month. Gravity would have to be extremely strong before you would notice a difference.

Black Holes—Gravity in the Extreme

Do such strong fields exist? Yes. But to produce such a field, you would need a lot of mass packed into a tiny volume of space. Although rare, such massive objects do occur as certain types of stars that have collapsed in on themselves.

A star such as our Sun doesn't collapse due to its own grav-ity because there is a balance between two forces throughout most of its life. While its mass of gases is pulled inward toward its center by gravity, at the same time all those gases are prevented from tumbling down into the core region by an upward pressure generated by the nuclear furnace at its center. This furnace turns hydrogen into helium and keeps the star shining. But like any fur-nace, it keeps needing more fuel, and a star like the Sun has only so much hydrogen fuel. Eventually all its usable fuel is burned up, and when this happens the star will be overcome by its own grav-ity and collapse. Without enough pressure in the core region to hold them up, the outer gases will tumble toward the center. In the case of the Sun, eventually a new force, called *degeneracy pressure*, will balance the gravity when the Sun has shrunk to about the size of Earth. A much more massive star will collapse so forcefully that nothing will be able to stop it.

When a star much more massive than the Sun collapses in this way, all that is left is a tiny black ball only a few miles across. All its matter is now packed into a compressed point at its center. This strange object is what we call a *black hole*. If you got very close to it you would find its gravitational field unbelievably strong.

Falling into a Black Hole

The "surface" of a black hole is called its *event horizon*, but it is not like the surface of a planet, but more like a boundary. You could pass right through it and hardly feel a thing, but once inside, you would never be able to get out again.

Let's try to imagine what it would be like to fall into a black hole. Assume you are in a spaceship at some distance from one. Beside you is another spaceship, and the astronaut in it radios that he wants to go into the black hole to find out what's inside. Through a telescope you watch the large clock on the wall of his cabin as gravity pulls him faster and faster toward the black hole. The closer he gets, the slower his clock runs. Then, as his spaceship approaches the event horizon, his clock almost, but never completely, stops. And his spaceship never actually reaches the black hole's event horizon. Instead, it lingers on and on just outside of it. What's happening? As odd as it might seem, because of his slowing of time, from our point of view he will never get there.

This may seem strange, but even stranger is the tale the astronaut who goes into the black hole would tell. He would say that as he approached the black hole he found himself in a tunnel that took him to the event horizon in only a few seconds. And then—zoom—he continued on past the event horizon right into the interior of the black hole. What would happen to him there? He might end up being crushed at the center, but, hard to believe as it is, he might pass right through and come out at some distant place and time! In that case he would have passed through what theorists call a *wormhole*.

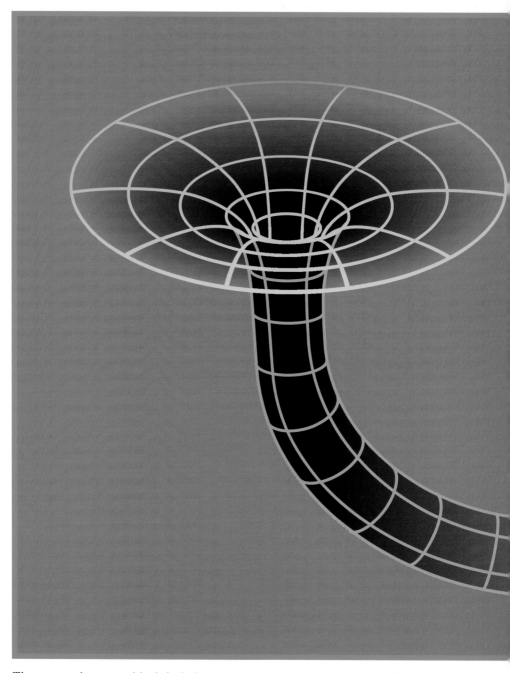

The space close to a black hole becomes so curved that it eventually takes on the form of a wormhole. If you got too close to it, you would be pulled inside. The wormhole has

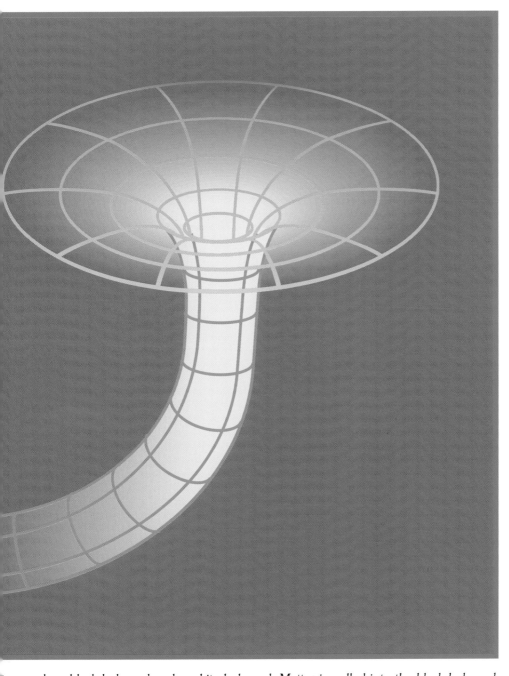

two ends: a black-hole end and a white-hole end. Matter is pulled into the black-hole end, and expelled out of the white-hole end.

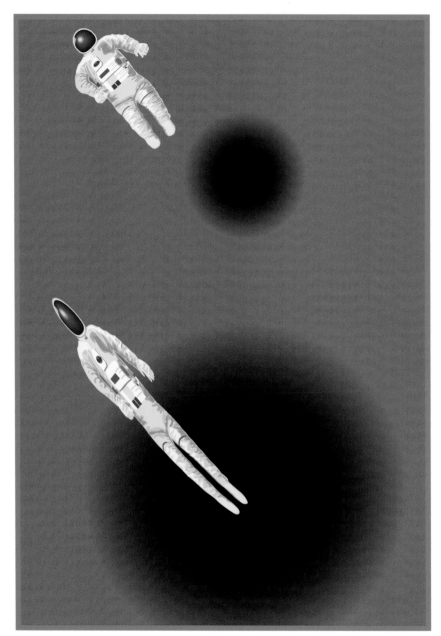

If you fell into a black hole, you would be gripped by strong gravitational tidal forces. The closer you got to the black hole, the stronger these forces would tug on you, stretching you out. Eventually, you would look like a piece of string because the gravitational forces would be greater at your feet than at your head.

Some astronomers think that such cosmic wormholes actually exist and serve as tunnels to other parts of the Universe. The Universe is so large and the stars so far apart that it is unlikely that we'll ever be able to visit them using ordinary spaceships. Wormholes may be the only way we'll be able to make such journeys, but that is not likely to occur for thousands of years. However, there may be civilizations out in space using them right now.

Depending on how large the black hole was, an imaginary astronaut might experience what are called *gravitational tidal forces*. These forces are so strong that they pull things apart. As the astronaut approached the black hole, the gravitational pull on the front of his spaceship would be greater than that on the rear because the front would be closer to the black hole's center of gravity. Therefore, he and his spaceship would be stretched apart. If it were a small black hole he would end up looking like a piece of string. But if it were very large, these tidal forces would be weak and he would pass into the black hole without serious injury.

Future of the Universe

Both Newton's and Einstein's theories of gravitation tell us that the countless galaxies of stars and planetary systems of many of those stars are prevented from flying apart by the universal force of gravitation. Turn off gravitation and Earth, Venus, Mars, and the other planets would no longer be held gravitational captives of the Sun. All of them would go flying off in straight-line paths. They would continue to flee until the gravitational force of some other star changed their straight-line courses.

In 1929, Edwin Hubble of Mount Wilson Observatory in California discovered that all galaxies are fleeing from us.

Indeed, he later showed that the entire Universe of galaxies is flying apart. According to most astronomers, the Universe was born in a gigantic explosion called the *Big Bang* that occurred about 15 billion years ago. From that moment, when time, space, and the formation of matter began, gravity has pretty much determined how the Universe has behaved. Astronomers tell us that gravitation will continue to control much of what happens until the end of the Universe— if it ever ends.

Edwin Hubble showed that the galaxies of the Universe are all moving away from one another. To us it appears that they are all moving away from Earth, but they would appear to be moving away from you regardless of where you were in the Universe.

Since all galaxies are rushing away from all the others, our galaxy, the Milky Way, is also moving away from all the others. All the while gravitation is tugging at the galaxies, tending to slow them down. An important question for astronomers is whether gravitation is strong enough to slow down and eventually stop the galaxies from moving apart. If it is, the expansion will stop and the Universe will collapse back in on itself. The gravitational pull on the galaxies depends on how much matter there is in the Universe. Is there enough to stop the expansion? Right now we don't know because some of the mass in the Universe seems to be in very strange forms. Astronomers call it *dark matter*. There are many possible forms of dark matter. Brown dwarf stars, black holes, and unusual types of particles are only a few of the possibilities. Vera Rubin of the Carnegie Institution of Washington is a leading authority on dark matter. She discovered that many galaxies have dark-matter "halos" by studying the motion of the visible stars in them.

Astronomers are still not certain if there is enough matter to stop the expansion of the Universe, but they think it is very close. If there is not quite enough matter, the Universe will continue expanding forever, with the galaxies getting farther and farther apart. If there is enough, on the other hand, the Universe will stop expanding and collapse down to a tiny very dense point in a process that astronomers call the *Big Crunch*. Perhaps that will set off another Big Bang, producing a new Universe.

Recently a number of astronomers have found evidence that the expansion of the Universe is not slowing down, but speeding up. If true, the galaxies are being pushed apart by some unknown force—a force of antigravity. It's a new and

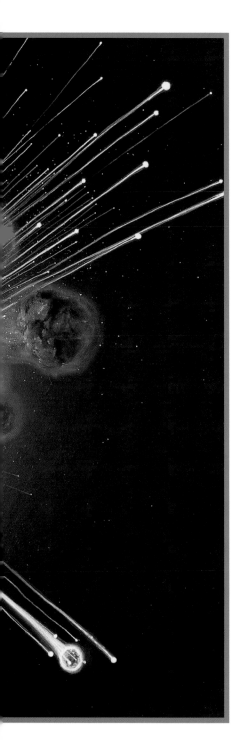

This is what the "Big Bang" might have looked like. It occurred about 15 billion years ago, when all the matter of the Universe was in a tiny "nucleus." Suddenly the Universe exploded, and gradually galaxies formed from the matter that was created and blown out. Our galaxy, the Milky Way, is one of these galaxies. Even though the galaxies are moving away from one another, gravity is still tugging at them, slowing them down. Or, an antigravity force may be pushing them ever farther apart, according to some astronomers.

Astronomer Vera Rubin has shown that there is a lot of "dark matter" hovering around galaxies. Although we cannot see it, we can see the effects of its gravitational pull.

strange idea, and it may be years before we know for sure if such a force actually exists.

Gravity is indeed strange. Newton gave us the first theory of gravitation but it left much unexplained. Einstein gave us a better theory that explained many of the things that Newton's theory left out. But even now we still do not thoroughly understand gravity.

Acceleration—any change in velocity.

Acceleration of gravity—the acceleration that a gravitational field produces when an object falls within it. In Earth's gravitational field, the acceleration is 32 feet (10 m) per second per second.

Antigravity—the opposite of gravity; a force that would cause two objects to repel one another.

Apparent brightness—the observed brightness of a star or other luminous object. The more distant an object, the dimmer it appears.

Big Bang—the explosion that is thought to have created the Universe about 15 billion years ago.

Big Crunch—the collapse of the Universe, which may occur if the Universe contains enough matter.

Black hole—the remains of a very massive star that has collapsed. The gravity at its surface is so strong that no light can escape from it.

Dark matter—matter in the Universe that cannot be seen but is detected through its gravitational effects.

Degeneracy pressure—the pressure exerted by a gas that has been squeezed to its "atomic" limit.

Ellipse—an oval-shaped curve.

Event horizon—the "surface" of a black hole.

Fifth essence—the material of stars and other heavenly bodies, as proposed by Aristotle.

Force—a push or pull exerted on a body.

Gravitation—the force of attraction acting between two objects.

Gravitational field—the field of force around any massive body; the greater the mass, the greater the gravitational field.

Gravitational tidal force—a gravitational force that changes over the length of a body, causing a stretching of the body.

Inertia—the resistance to change in motion; the tendency of an object to continue at the same speed and in the same direction unless acted upon by a force.

Inertial field—the field that is generated when a body accelerates, the field being equivalent to a gravitational field.

Inertial force—the force acting on a body when the motion of the body is changed.

Wormhole—a region of extremely curved space; a gravitational tunnel extending from a black hole and exiting into another Universe.

Caspar, Max. *Johannes Kepler*. New York: Dover, 1993.

Ferguson, Kitty. *Measuring the Universe*. New York: Walker and Co., 1999.

Koestler, Arthur. *The Watershed*. Lantham, MD: University Press of America, 1984.

Parker, Barry. *Cosmic Time Travel*. New York: Plenum Press, 1991.

_____. *Einstein's Dream*. New York: Plenum Press, 1986.

_____. *The Vindication of the Big Bang*. New York: Plenum Press, 1993.

Reston, James Jr. *Galileo: A Life*. New York: HarperCollins, 1994.

Westfall, Richard. *Never at Rest: A Biography of Isaac Newton*. Cambridge: Cambridge University Press, 1980.

Index

Page numbers for illustrations are in **boldface**.

About the Author

Barry Parker is a professor emeritus of physics and astronomy at Idaho State University. He is the author of seventeen books, including *Einstein's Brainchild*, *Cosmic Time Travel*, *Alien Life*, *Colliding Galaxies*, and *Einstein's Dream*. He has also written for other publications, including *Encyclopedia Britannica*, *The Washington Post*, *Time-Life Books*, and *Astronomy* magazine. He taught physics and astronomy at Idaho State University until his retirement in 1997, and he also did research on Einstein's theories, and in other areas. He lives in Pocatello, Idaho.